Silly Millies

Make Sense!

Jean Haddon

illustrated by **Carl DiRocco**

M Millbrook Press   Minneapolis

For Abby

Text copyright © 2007 by Jean Haddon

Illustrations copyright © 2007 by Millbrook Press, Inc.

Millbrook Press, Inc.
A division of Lerner Publishing Group
241 First Avenue North
Minneapolis, Minnesota 55401 U.S.A.

Website address: www.lernerbooks.com

Library of Congress Cataloging-in-Publication Data

Haddon, Jean.
    Make sense! / by Jean Haddon ; illustrated by Carl Di Rocco.
       p. cm. — (Silly Millies)
    ISBN-13: 978-0-7613-3403-3 (lib. bdg. : alk. paper)
    ISBN-10: 0-7613-3403-3 (lib. bdg. : alk. paper)
    1. Senses and sensation—Juvenile literature. I. Title. II. Series.
QP434.H33 2007
612.8—dc22   2005011056

Manufactured in the United States of America
1 2 3 4 5 6 – DP – 12 11 10 09 08 07

Can you **taste** a skunk?

Can you **hear** a rose?

Can you **see**
a nice smell?

Make **sense**....

Use your **NOSE!**

Can you **smell** an opera?

Can you **taste** loud cheers?

Can you **touch** thunder?

BOOM! BOOM!

Make **sense**....

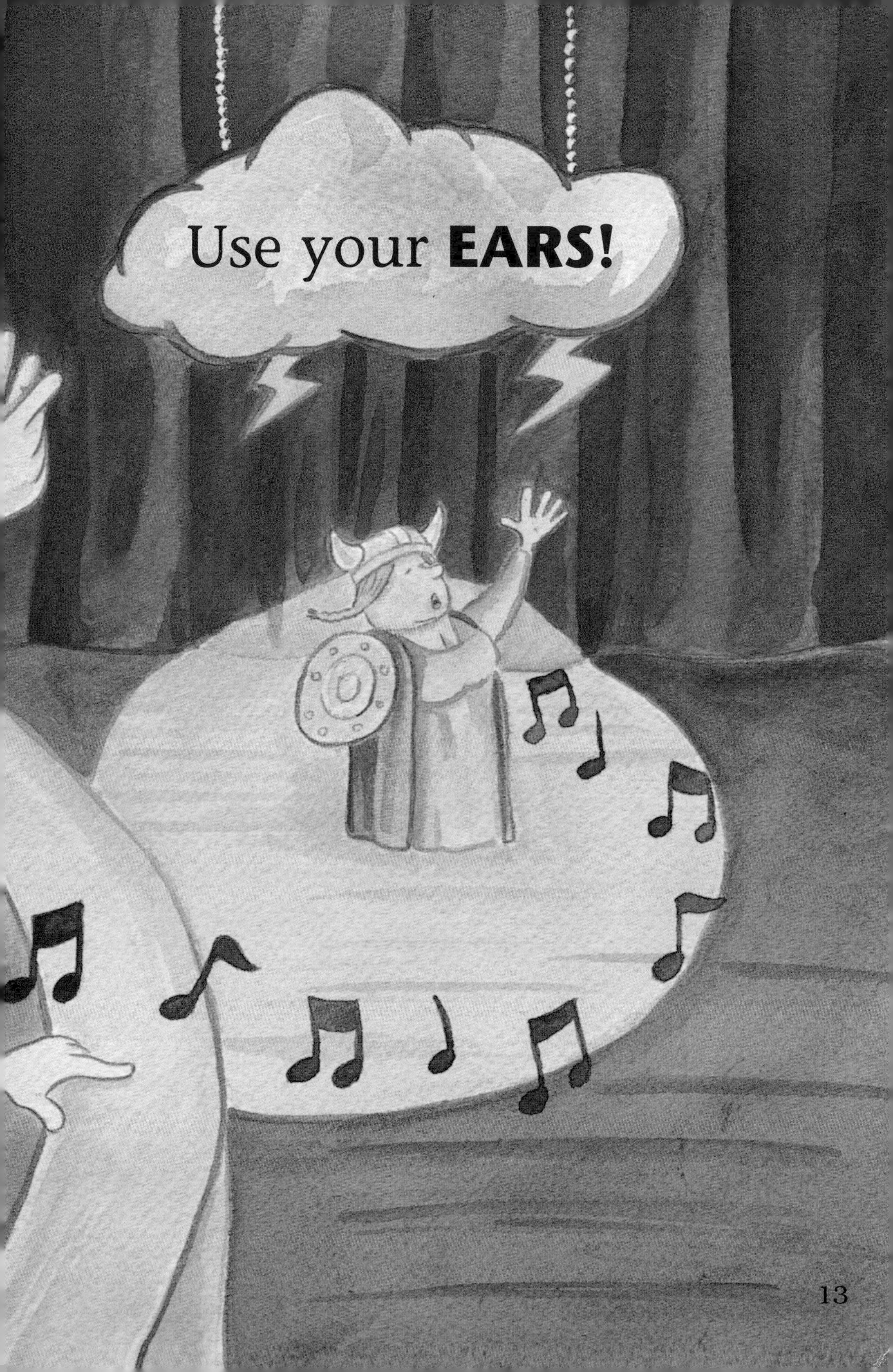

Use your **EARS!**

Can you **hear** a painting?

Can you **taste** the blue skies?

Can you **touch** a rainbow?

Make **sense**....

Use your **EYES!**

Can you **hear**
your towel?

(It won't say much.)

Can you **taste** your doggie?

Make **sense**....

Use your **TOUCH!**

Can you **smell** a spoon?

Can you **hear** your toothpaste?

Can you just **look** at
ice cream?

Maybe not....

Use your **TASTE!**

Tips for Discussion

Go back through the book, looking at all the silly ways that senses are being used. Name what sense should **really** be used for each of the silly examples.

Can you name more ways it would make sense to be using your ears or your eyes, or your other senses?

Make your own list of silly ways to use each of the senses, for example, tasting a rock or touching a dream.

Can you think of things for which you would use more than one of your senses? Examples are seeing and hearing fireworks, or smelling and tasting some fresh-baked cookies.

About the Author

Jean Haddon lives in Connecticut, where she does her best to smell the roses instead of the skunks. She is still waiting for the day when everything will make sense. In the meantime, she has written two other Silly Millies, *Words* and *It's a Beautiful Day*.